D0246973

THE USBORNE
CHILDREN'S
SONGBOOK

Compiled by Heather Amery
Illustrated by Stephen Cartwright

Music arrangements by Caroline Hooper

Music setting by David Kear

 There are some little yellow ducks to spot in this book.
How many can you spot?

ABERDEENSHIRE COUNCIL

J784,624
620676

Revised edition first published in 1997 by Usborne Publishing Ltd, Usborne House, 83-85 Saffron Hill,
London, EC1N 8RT, England.
Copyright © 1997, 1988 Usborne Publishing Ltd.

The name Usborne and the device are Trade Marks of Usborne Publishing Ltd.

All rights reserved. No part of this publication may be reproduced, stored in a retrieval system, or
transmitted in any form or by any means, electronic, mechanical, photocopying, recording or otherwise,
without the prior permission of the publisher. Printed in Great Britain.

Every effort has been made to trace the copyright owners. If any right has been omitted, the publishers
offer their apologies and will rectify this in any subsequent editions following notification.

Contents

Here we go round the mulberry bush

Andante

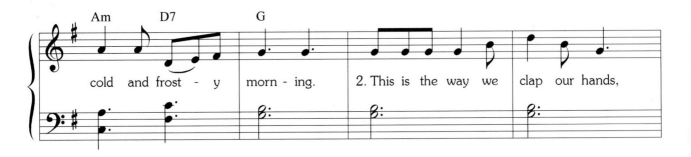

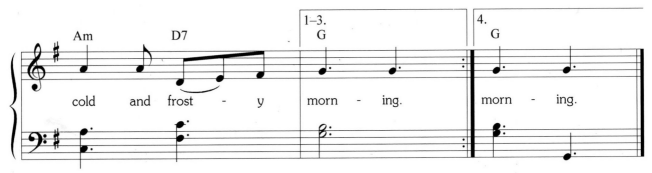

1 Here we go round the mulberry bush,
The mulberry bush, the mulberry bush,
Here we go round the mulberry bush
On a cold and frosty morning.

2 This is the way we clap our hands,
Clap our hands, clap our hands,
This is the way we clap our hands
On a cold and frosty morning.

3 This is the way we wash our clothes,
Wash our clothes, wash our clothes,
This is the way we wash our clothes
On a cold and frosty morning.

4 This is the way we sweep the floor,
Sweep the floor, sweep the floor,
This is the way we sweep the floor
On a cold and frosty morning.

You can make up some verses of your own for this song, like comb your hair,
brush your teeth and wash your face.

One, two, three, four, five

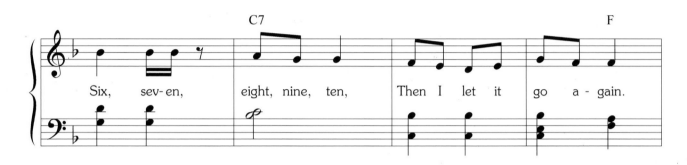

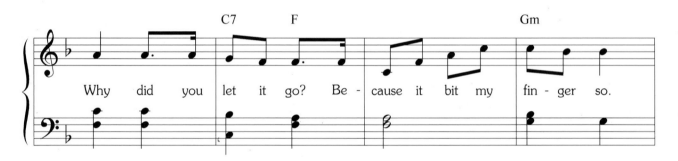

1 One, two, three, four, five,
   Once I caught a fish alive;
   Six, seven, eight, nine, ten,
   Then I let it go again.

2 Why did you let it go?
   Because it bit my finger so.
   Which finger did it bite?
   This little finger on the right.

Little Bo-Peep

1   Little Bo-Peep has lost her sheep
And doesn't know where to find them.
Leave them alone, and they'll come home,
Wagging their tails behind them.

      2   It happened one day, as Bo-Peep did stray
Into a meadow hard by,
There she spied their tails side by side,
All hung on a tree to dry.

           3   She heaved a sigh, and wiped her eye
And over the hillocks went rambling;
And tried what she could,
     as a shepherdess should,
To tack again each to its lambkin.

If you're happy

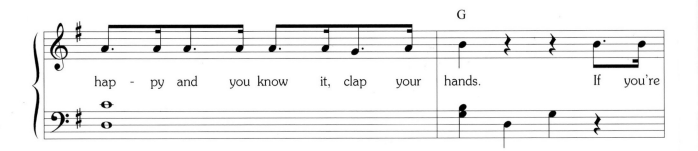

1   If you're happy and you know it, clap your hands.
    If you're happy and you know it, clap your hands.
    If you're happy and you know it, and you really want to show it,
    If you're happy and you know it, clap your hands.

2   If you're happy and you know it, nod your head...
3   If you're happy and you know it, stamp your feet...
4   If you're happy and you knu're it, say "Ha! Ha!"...
5   If you're happy and you know it, dó all four!...

8

Where, oh where has my little dog gone?

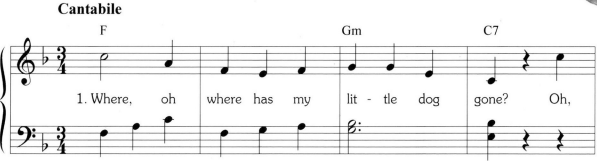

Cantabile

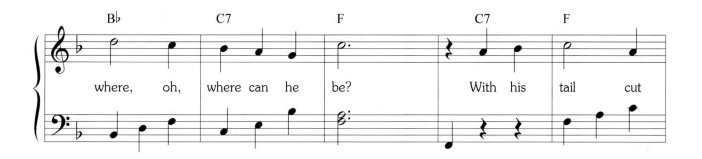

1. Where, oh where has my lit - tle dog gone? Oh,

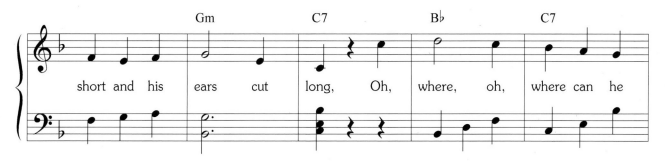

where, oh, where can he be? With his tail cut

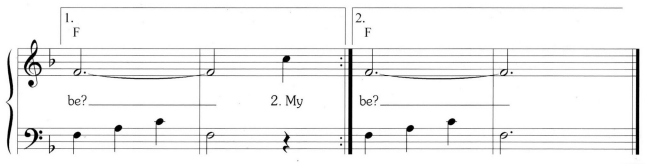

short and his ears cut long, Oh, where, oh, where can he

1. F
be? _____ 2. My

2. F
be? _____

1   Where, oh where has my little dog gone?
    Oh where, oh where can he be?
    With his tail cut short and his ears cut long,
    Oh where, oh where can he be?

2   My little dog always waggles his tail
    Whenever he wants his grog.
    And if the tail were more strong than he,
    Why, the tail would waggle the dog.

9

Ten in a bed

Allegro

1. There were ten in the bed And the lit - tle one said, "Roll

o - ver! Roll o - ver!" So they all rolled o - ver and

1–8.
one fell out. 2. There were

9.
one fell out. 10. There was

one in the bed And this lit-tle one said, "Good - night. Good - night."

1 There were ten in the bed
   And the little one said,
   "Roll over! Roll over!"
   So they all rolled over and one fell out.

2 There were nine in the bed
       And the little one said...

3 There were eight in the bed
       And the little one said...

4 There were seven in the bed
       And the little one said...

5 There were six in the bed
       And the little one said...

6 There were five in the bed
       And the little one said...

7 There were four in the bed
       And the little one said...

8 There were three in the bed
       And the little one said...

9 There were two in the bed
       And the little one said...

10 There was one in the bed
   And this little one said,
   "Good night. Good night."

Twinkle, twinkle, little star

Dolce

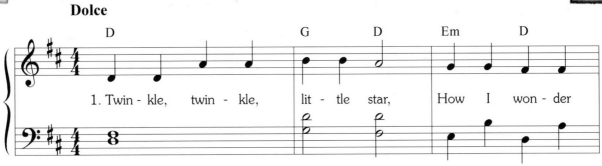

1. Twin - kle, twin - kle, lit - tle star, How I won - der

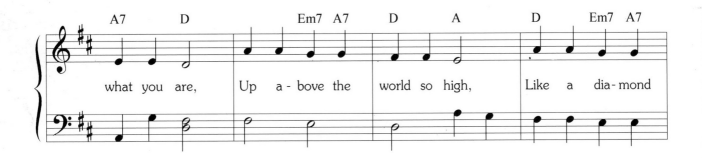

what you are, Up a - bove the world so high, Like a dia - mond

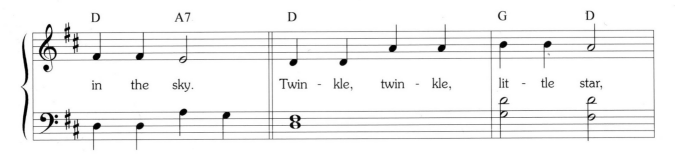

in the sky. Twin - kle, twin - kle, lit - tle star,

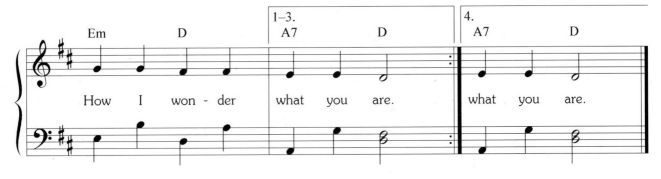

How I won - der   what you are.   what you are.

1 Twinkle, twinkle, little star,
  How I wonder what you are,
  Up above the world so high,
  Like a diamond in the sky.
      Twinkle, twinkle, little star,
      How I wonder what you are.

2 When the blazing sun is gone,
  When he nothing shines upon,
  Then you show your little light,
  Twinkle, twinkle, all the night.
      Twinkle, twinkle, little star,
      How I wonder what you are.

3 Then the traveller in the dark
  Thanks you for your tiny spark.
  Could he see which way to go
  If you did not twinkle so?
      Twinkle, twinkle, little star,
      How I wonder what you are.

4 In the dark blue sky you keep,
  And often through my curtains peep.
  For you never shut your eye
  Till the sun is in the sky.
      Twinkle, twinkle, little star,
      How I wonder what you are.

Old MacDonald had a farm

Allegro

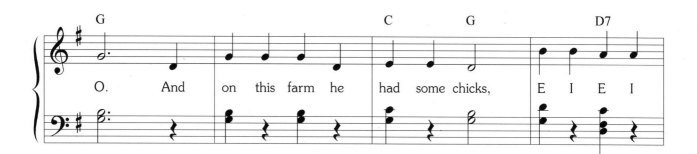

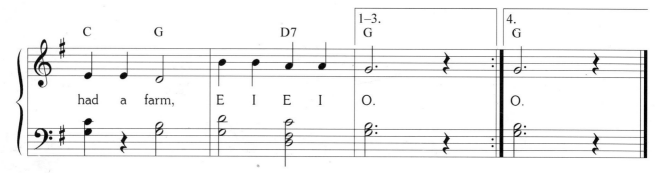

1   Old MacDonald had a farm, E I E I O.
And on this farm he had some chicks, E I E I O.
With a chick-chick here and a chick-chick there,
Here a chick, there a chick, everywhere a chick-chick.
Old MacDonald had a farm, E I E I O.

2   Old MacDonald had a farm, E I E I O.
And on this farm he had some ducks, E I E I O.
With a quack-quack here and a quack-quack there,
Here a quack, there a quack, everywhere a quack-quack.
Old MacDonald had a farm, E I E I O.

3   Old MacDonald had a farm, E I E I O.
And on this farm he had some sheep, E I E I O.
With a baa-baa here and a baa-baa there,
Here a baa, there a baa, everywhere a baa-baa.
Old MacDonald had a farm, E I E I O.

4   Old MacDonald had a farm, E I E I O.
And on this farm he had some pigs, E I E I O.
With a grunt-grunt here and a grunt-grunt there,
Here a grunt, there a grunt, everywhere a grunt-grunt.
Old MacDonald had a farm, E I E I O.

I had a little nut tree

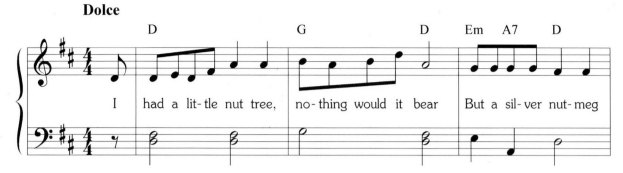

Dolce

I had a lit-tle nut tree, no-thing would it bear But a sil-ver nut-meg

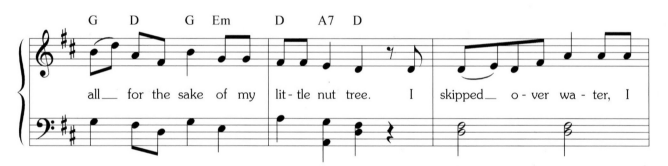

and a gold-en pear. The King of Spain's daugh-ter came to vis-it me, And

all for the sake of my lit-tle nut tree. I skipped o-ver wa-ter, I

danced o-ver sea, And all the birds in the air could-n't catch me.

I had a little nut tree, nothing would it bear,
But a silver nutmeg and a golden pear.
The King of Spain's daughter came to visit me,
And all for the sake of my little nut tree.
I skipped over water, I danced over sea,
And all the birds in the air couldn't catch me.

16

Frère Jacques

Andante

F

Frè – re Jac – ques, frè – re Jac – ques,

Dor – mez – vous? Dor – mez – vous?

Son – nez les ma – ti – nes, Son – nez les ma – ti – nes,

Ding, dingue, dong! Ding, dingue, dong!

Frère Jacques, Frère Jacques,
Dormez-vous? Dormez-vous?
Sonnez les matines,
Sonnez les matines,
Ding, dingue, dong! Ding, dingue, dong!

This old man

Allegro

1. This old man, he played one, He played nick - nack

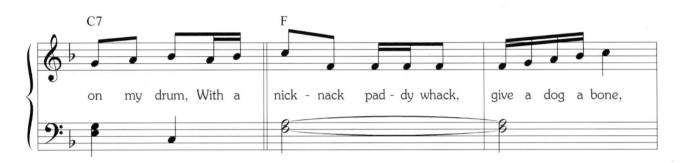

on my drum, With a nick - nack pad - dy whack, give a dog a bone,

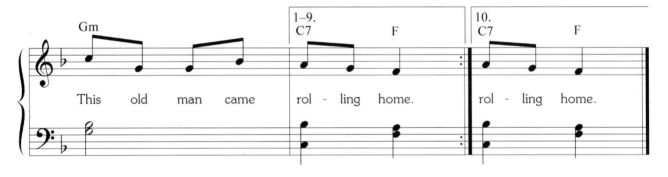

This old man came rol - ling home. rol - ling home.

1   This old man, he played one,
He played nick-nack on my drum.
With a nick-nack, paddy whack, give a dog a bone,
This old man came rolling home.

2 This old man, he played two,
   He played nick-nack on my shoe.
       With a nick-nack, paddy whack...

3 This old man, he played three,
   He played nick-nack on my tree.
       With a nick-nack, paddy whack...

4 This old man, he played four,
   He played nick-nack on my door.
       With a nick-nack, paddy whack...

5 This old man, he played five,
   He played nick-nack on my hive.
       With a nick-nack, paddy whack...

6 This old man, he played six,
   He played nick-nack on my sticks.
       With a nick-nack, paddy whack...

7 This old man, he played seven,
   He played nick-nack up in heaven.
       With a nick-nack, paddy whack

8 This old man, he played eight,
   He played nick-nack on my gate.
       With a nick-nack, paddy whack...

9 This old man, he played nine,
   He played nick-nack on my line.
       With a nick-nack, paddy whack...

10 This old man, he played ten,
   He played nick-nack on my hen.
       With a nick-nack, paddy whack...

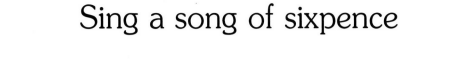

Sing a song of sixpence

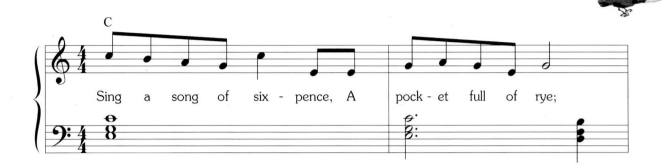

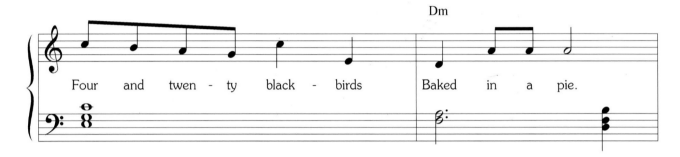

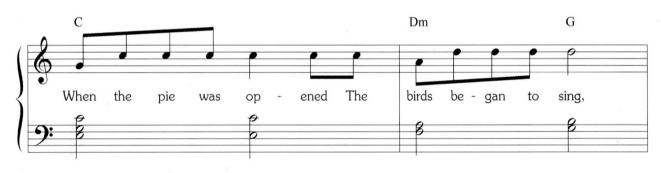

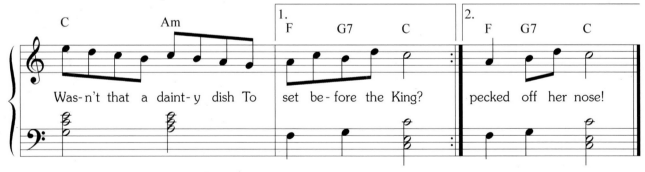

1 Sing a song of sixpence,
   A pocket full of rye;
   Four and twenty blackbirds
   Baked in a pie.

2 When the pie was opened
   The birds began to sing,
   Wasn't that a dainty dish
   To set before the King?

3 The King was in his counting-house,
   Counting out his money;
   The Queen was in the parlour,
   Eating bread and honey;

4 The maid was in the garden,
   Hanging out the clothes,
   When down came a blackbird
   And pecked off her nose.

Jingle bells

Vivace

1. Dash-ing through the snow In a one-horse o-pen sleigh, O'er the fields we go, Laugh-ing all the way; Bells on bob-tail ring, Mak-ing spi-rits bright; What fun it is to ride and sing A sleigh-ing song to-night. Oh,

Dashing through the snow
In a one-horse open sleigh,
O'er the fields we go,
Laughing all the way.
Bells on bob-tail ring,
Making spirits bright;
What fun it is to ride and sing
A sleighing song tonight.

Oh, jingle bells, jingle bells,
Jingle all the way.
Oh what fun it is to ride
In a one-horse open sleigh.
Oh, jingle bells, jingle bells,
Jingle all the way.
Oh what fun it is to ride
In a one-horse open sleigh.

jin-gle bells, jin-gle bells, Jin-gle all the way. Oh what fun it is to ride In a

one-horse o-pen sleigh. Oh, jin-gle bells, jin-gle bells, Jin-gle all the way.

Oh what fun it is to ride In a one-horse o-pen sleigh. one-horse o-pen sleigh.

A day or two ago
I thought I'd take a ride
And soon Miss Fannie Bright
Was seated by my side;
The horse was lean and lank,
Misfortune seem'd his lot,
He got into a drifted bank,
And then we got upsot!

Oh, jingle bells, jingle bells,
Jingle all the way.
Oh what fun it is to ride
In a one-horse open sleigh.
Oh, jingle bells, jingle bells,
Jingle all the way.
Oh what fun it is to ride
In a one-horse open sleigh.

Michael Finnigan

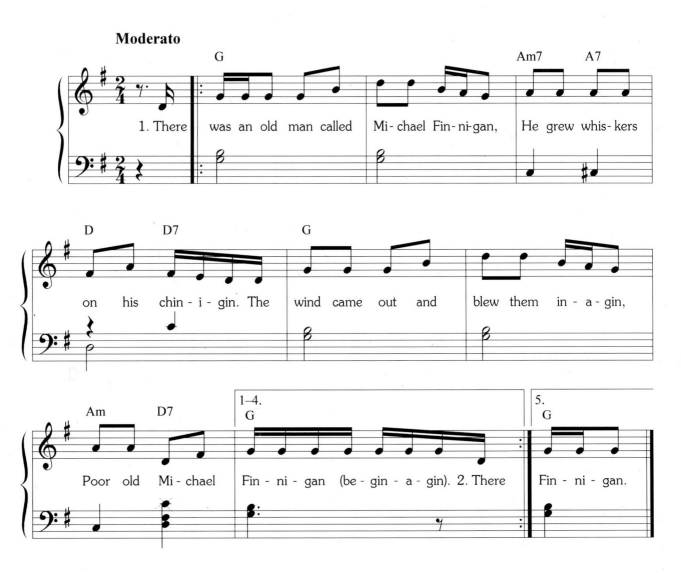

1. There was an old man called Michael Finnigan,
He grew whiskers on his chinigin.
The wind came out and blew them inagin,
Poor old Michael Finnigan (beginagin).

2 There was an old man called Michael Finnigan,
   He kicked up an awful dinigin,
   Because they said he must not singagin,
   Poor old Michael Finnigan (beginagin).

3 There was an old man called Michael Finnigan,
   He went fishing with a pinigin,
   Caught a fish but dropped it inagin,
   Poor old Michael Finnigan (beginagin).

4 There was an old man called Michael Finnigan,
   Climbed a tree and barked his shinigin,
   Took off several yards of skinigin,
   Poor old Michael Finnigan (beginagin).

5 There was an old man called Michael Finnigan,
   He grew fat and he grew thinagin,
   Then he died, and we have to beginagin,
   Poor old Michael Finnigan, Finnigan.

I saw three ships

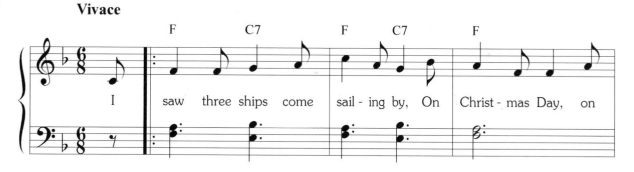

Vivace

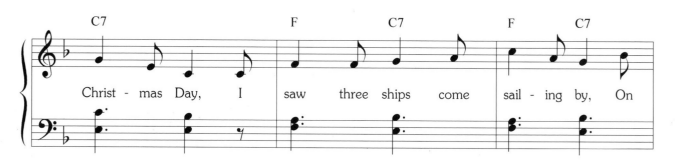

I saw three ships come sail-ing by, On Christ-mas Day, on

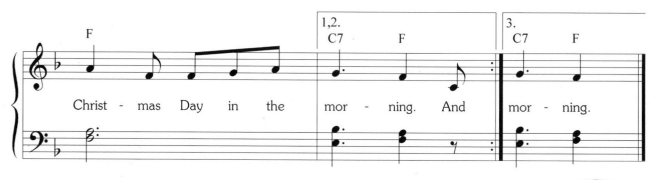

Christ-mas Day, I saw three ships come sail-ing by, On

Christ-mas Day in the mor-ning. And mor-ning.

1 I saw three ships come sailing by,
  On Christmas Day, on Christmas Day,
  I saw three ships come sailing by,
  On Christmas Day in the morning.

2 And what was in those ships all three?
  On Christmas Day, on Christmas Day,
  And what was in those ships all three?
  On Christmas Day in the morning.

3 Our Saviour Christ and his lady.
  On Christmas Day, on Christmas Day,
  Our Saviour Christ and his lady.
  On Christmas Day in the morning.

Yankee Doodle

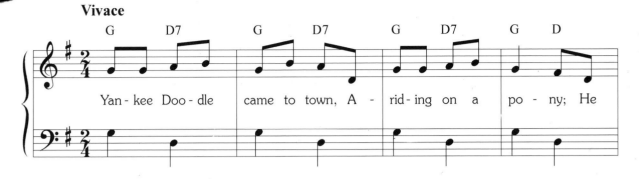

1 Yankee Doodle came to town,
   A-riding on a pony;
   He stuck a feather in his cap
   And called it macaroni.

2 Yankee Doodle, keep it up,
   Yankee Doodle Dandy,
   Mind the music and the step,
   And with the girls be handy.

London Bridge is falling down

Allegro

1. Lon - don Bridge is fal - ling down, Fal - ling down, fal - ling down,

Lon - don Bridge is fal - ling down, My fair la - dy.

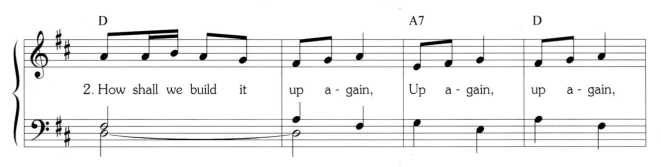

2. How shall we build it up a - gain, Up a - gain, up a - gain,

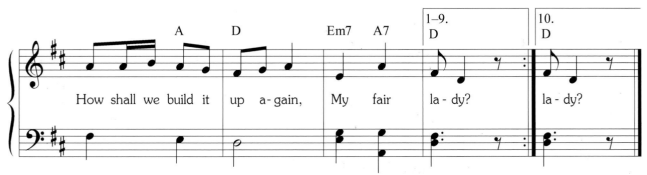

How shall we build it up a - gain, My fair la - dy? la - dy?

1 London Bridge is falling down,
   Falling down, falling down,
   London Bridge is falling down,
   My fair lady.

2 How shall we build it up again,
   Up again, up again,
   How shall we build it up again,
   My fair lady.

3 Build it up with silver and gold,
   Silver and gold, silver and gold...

4 Silver and gold will be stolen away
   Stolen away, stolen away...

5 Build it up with wood and clay,
   Wood and clay, wood and clay...

6 Wood and clay will wash away,
   Wash away, wash away...

7 Build it up with iron and steel,
   Iron and steel, iron and steel...

8 Iron and steel will bend and bow,
   Bend and bow, bend and bow...

9 Build it up with stone so strong,
   Stone so strong, stone so strong...

10 Stone will last for ages long,
   For ages long, for ages long...

Pop goes the weasel

Moderato

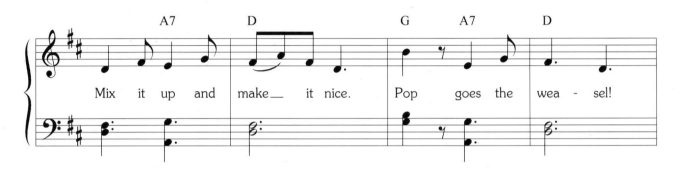

Half a pound of tup-pen-ny rice, Half a pound of trea - cle,

Mix it up and make__ it nice. Pop goes the wea - sel!

Up and down the Ci - ty Road, In and out the Ea - gle,

That's the way the mo - ney goes. Pop goes the wea - sel!

1 Half a pound of tuppenny rice,
   Half a pound of treacle,
   Mix it up and make it nice.
   Pop goes the weasel!

2 Up and down the City Road,
   In and out the Eagle,
   That's the way the money goes.
   Pop goes the weasel!

The grand old Duke of York

Moderato

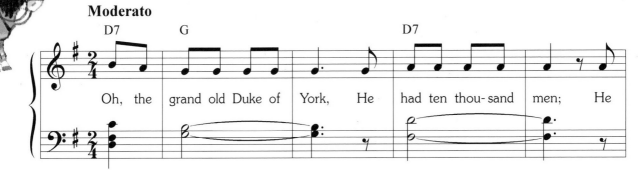

Oh, the | grand old Duke of | York, He | had ten thou-sand | men; He

marched them up to the | top of the hill And he | marched them down a - | gain. And

when they were up, they were | up; And | when they were down, they were | down; And

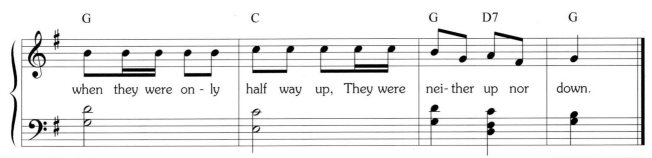

when they were on - ly | half way up, They were | nei-ther up nor | down.

1 Oh, the grand old Duke of York,
   He had ten thousand men;
   He marched them up to the top of the hill
   And he marched them down again.

2 And when they were up, they were up;
   And when they were down, they were down;
   And when they were only half way up,
   They were neither up nor down.

One more river

Moderato

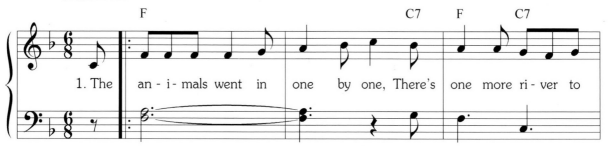

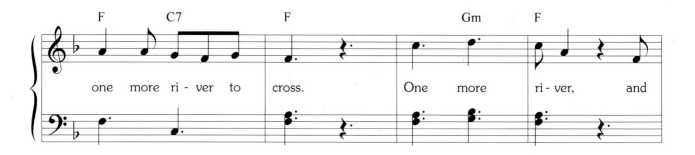

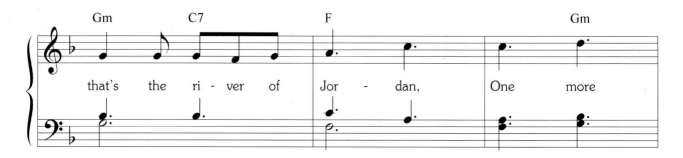

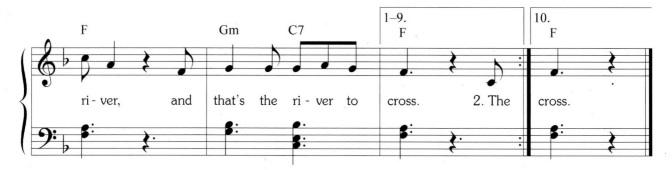

32

1 The animals went in one by one,
There's one more river to cross.
The elephant chewing a caraway bun,
There's one more river to cross.

One more river, and that's the river of Jordan
One more river, and that's the river to cross.

2 The animals went in two by two,
There's one more river to cross.
There's the crocodile and the kangaroo,
There's one more river to cross.
       One more river...

3 The animals went in three by three,
There's one more river to cross.
There's the tall giraffe and the tiny flea,
There's one more river to cross.
       One more river...

4 The animals went in four by four,
There's one more river to cross.
The big hippopotamus stuck in the door,
There's one more river to cross.
       One more river...

5 The animals went in five by five
There's one more river to cross.
The bees mistook the bear for a hive,
There's one more river to cross.
       One more river...

More verses to sing:
6   The monkey was up to his usual tricks...
7   Said the ant to the antelope, "Who are you shovin'?"...
8   Some were early and some were late...
9   They all formed fours and marched in a line...
10 If you want any more you can sing it again...

Click go the shears

Moderato

1. Down by the pen, there the old shear - er stands,

Grasp - ing the shears___ in his thin bo - ny hands, Fixed is his gaze on the

next sheep to come, In a lit - tle min - ute, boys, a - no - ther's done.

1   Down by the pen, there the old shearer stands,
Grasping the shears in his thin bony hands,
Fixed is his gaze on the next sheep to come,
In a little minute, boys, another's done.

Click go the shears, boys, click, click, click.
Wide is his blow and his hands move so quick.
The ringer looks around and is beaten by a blow,
Zip! Another sheep is done and let him go.

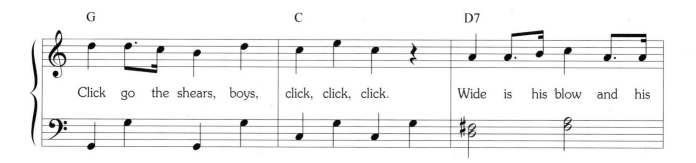

Click go the shears, boys, click, click, click. Wide is his blow and his

hands move so quick. The ring-er looks a-round and is beat-en by a blow,

Zip! A-no-ther sheep is done and let him go. let him go.

2 Out on the floor in his cane bottomed chair,
   There sits the boss with his eyes everywhere,
   Notes well each fleece as it comes to the screen,
   Paying strict attention that it's taken clean.

   Click go the shears, boys,...

3 There is the tar-boy awaiting his command
   With his black tar pot and his black tarry hands.
   See! One old sheep with a cut on its back.
   Here is what he's waiting for, it's tar here, Jack.

   Click go the shears, boys,...

35

My bonnie lies over the ocean

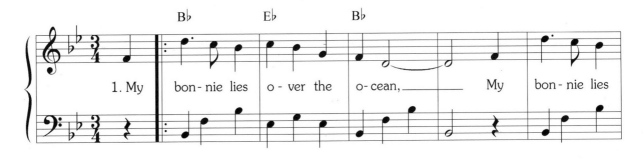

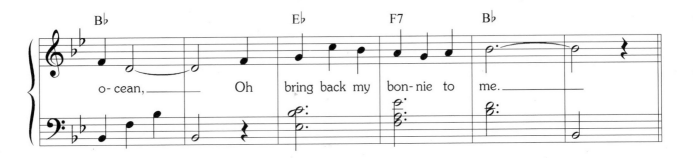

1   My bonnie lies over the ocean,
     My bonnie lies over the sea,
     My bonnie lies over the ocean,
     Oh bring back my bonnie to me.

Bring back, bring back,
Oh bring back my bonnie to me, to me.
Bring back, bring back,
Oh bring back my bonnie to me.

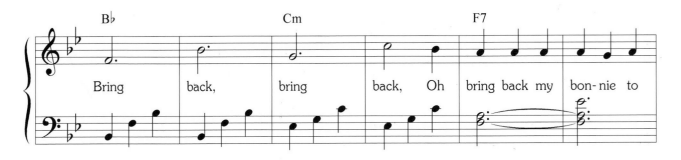

Bb   Cm   F7

Bring   back,   bring   back,   Oh   bring back my   bon-nie to

Bb   Eb   Cm

me,   to   me.   Bring   back,   bring   back,   Oh

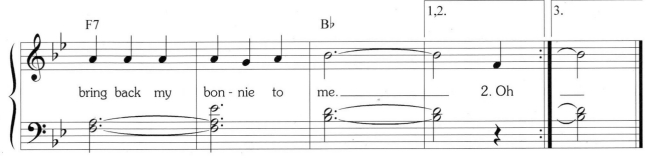

F7   Bb   1,2.   3.

bring back my   bon-nie to   me.   2. Oh

2   Oh blow ye winds over the ocean,
Oh blow ye winds over the sea,
Oh blow ye winds over the ocean,
And bring back my bonnie to me.
Bring back, bring back...

3   The winds have blown over the ocean,
The winds have blown over the sea,
The winds have blown over the ocean,
And brought back my bonnie to me.
Bring back, bring back...

She'll be coming round the mountain

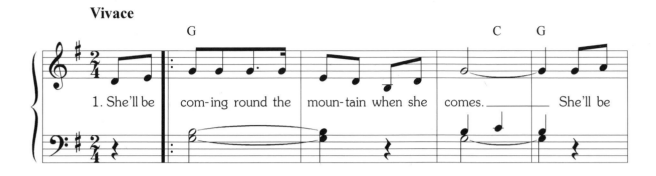

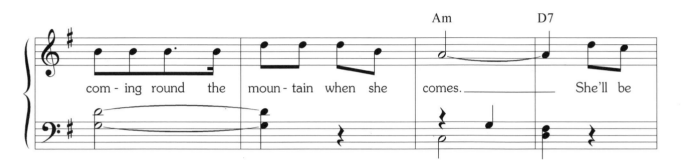

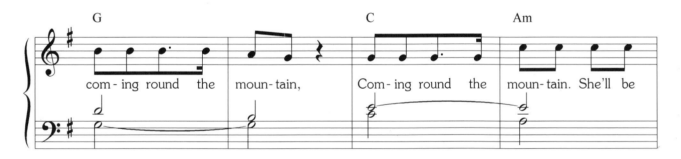

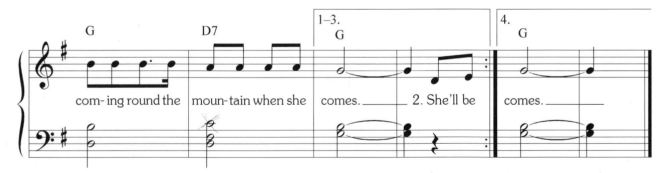

1 She'll be coming round the mountain when she comes.
She'll be coming round the mountain when she comes.
She'll be coming round the mountain,
Coming round the mountain.
She'll be coming round the mountain when she comes.

2 She'll be driving six white horses when she comes.
She'll be driving six white horses when she comes.
She'll be driving six white horses,
Driving six white horses.
She'll be driving six white horses when she comes.

3 Oh we'll all go out and greet her when she comes.
Oh we'll all go out and greet her when she comes.
Oh we'll all go out and greet her,
All go out and greet her.
Oh we'll all go out and greet her when she comes.

4 But it may be just a while yet 'fore she comes.
Yes, it may be just a while yet 'fore she comes.
Oh, it may be just a while yet,
May be just a while yet.
Yes it may be just a while yet 'fore she comes.

There's a big ship sailing

Andante

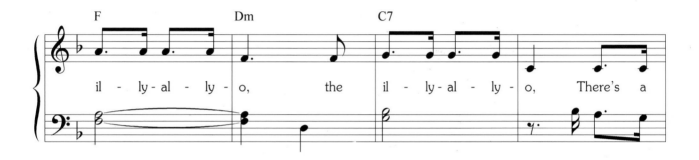

1. There's a big ship sail - ing on the il - ly-al - ly - o, The

il - ly-al - ly - o, the il - ly-al - ly - o, There's a

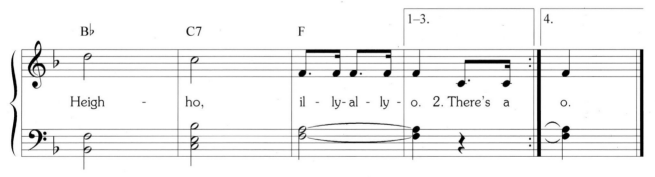

big ship sail - ing on the il - ly-al - ly - o,

Heigh - ho, il - ly-al - ly - o. 2. There's a o.

40

1 There's a big ship sailing on the illy-ally-o,
  The illy-ally-o, the illy-ally-o,
  There's a big ship sailing on the illy-ally-o,
  Heigh-ho, illy-ally-o.

2 There's a big ship sailing, rocking on the sea,
  Rocking on the sea, rocking on the sea,
  There's a big ship sailing, rocking on the sea,
  Heigh-ho, rocking on the sea.

3 The Captain said, "It'll never, never do,
  Never, never do, never, never do,"
  The Captain said, "It'll never, never do,
  Heigh-ho, never, never do."

4 The big ship sank to the bottom of the sea,
  The bottom of the sea, the bottom of the sea,
  The big ship sank to the bottom of the sea,
  Heigh-ho, the bottom of the sea.

Cockles and mussels

Cantabile

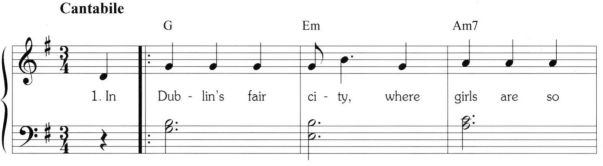

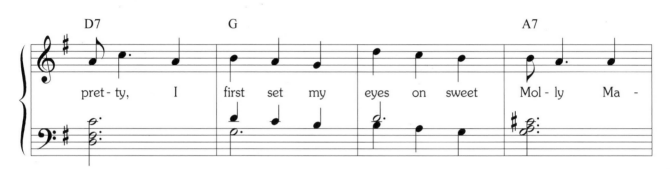

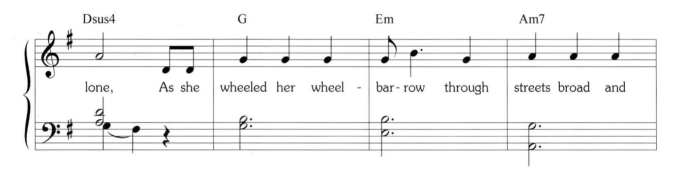

1   In Dublin's fair city, where girls are so pretty,
    I first set my eyes on sweet Molly Malone,
    As she wheeled her wheelbarrow through streets broad
       and narrow,
    Crying, "Cockles and mussels, alive, alive-o."

        Alive, alive-o, alive, alive-o,
        Crying "Cockles and mussels, alive alive-o."

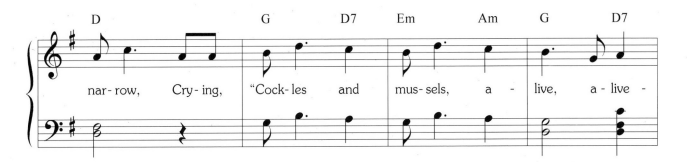

D   G D7 Em Am G   D7

nar-row, Cry-ing, "Cock-les and mus-sels, a - live, a - live -

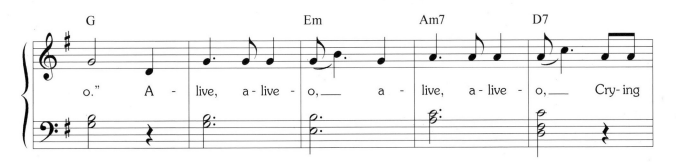

G   Em   Am7   D7

o." A - live, a - live - o,___ a - live, a - live - o,___ Cry-ing

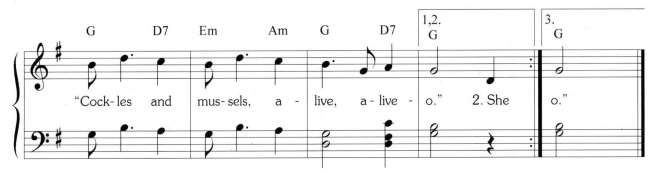

G D7 Em Am G D7   1,2.   3.
                   G   G

"Cock-les and mus-sels, a - live, a - live - o." 2. She o."

2 She was a fishmonger, but it was no wonder,
For so were her mother and father before,
And they each wheeled their barrow through streets broad
  and narrow,
Crying, "Cockles and mussels, alive, alive-o."
  Alive, alive-o, alive, alive-o…

3 She died of a fever, and no one could save her,
And that was the end of sweet Molly Malone,
Now her ghost wheels her barrow through streets broad
  and narrow,
Crying, "Cockles and mussels, alive, alive-o."
  Alive, alive-o, alive, alive-o…

Over the hills and far away

Moderato

1. Tom,__ he__ was a__ pi-per's son, He learnt__ to__ play__ when__

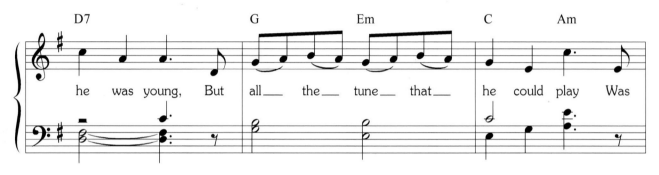

he was young, But all__ the__ tune__ that__ he could play Was

"O - ver the hills and far a - way". O - ver the hills and a

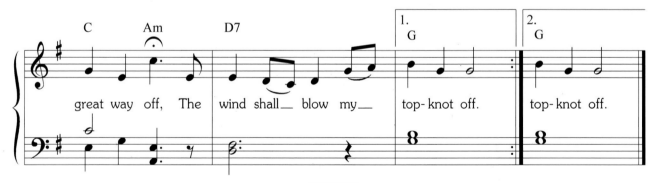

great way off, The wind shall__ blow my__ top-knot off. top-knot off.

1 Tom, he was a piper's son,
   He learnt to play when he was young,
   But all the tune that he could play
   Was "Over the hills and far away".
   Over the hills and a great way off,
   The wind will blow my top-knot off.

2 Tom with his pipe made such a noise,
   That he pleased both the girls and boys,
   And they all stopped to hear him play,
   "Over the hills and far away".
   Over the hills and a great way off,
   The wind will blow my top-knot off.

3 Tom played his pipe with such good will
   That those who heard him could ne'er keep still;
   As soon as he played they began to dance,
   E'en pigs on their hind legs began to prance.
   Over the hills and a great way off,
   The wind will blow my top-knot off.

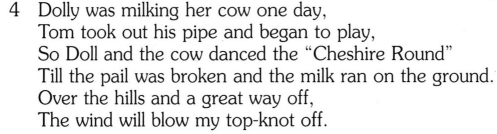

4 Dolly was milking her cow one day,
   Tom took out his pipe and began to play,
   So Doll and the cow danced the "Cheshire Round"
   Till the pail was broken and the milk ran on the ground.
   Over the hills and a great way off,
   The wind will blow my top-knot off.

Au clair de la lune

Moderato

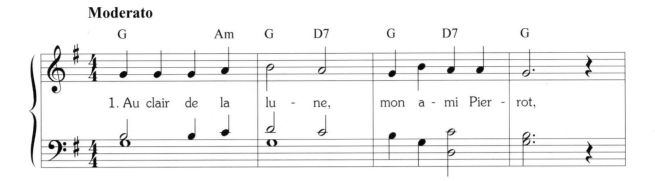

1. Au clair de la lu - ne, mon a - mi Pier - rot,

Prê - te - moi ta plu - me, pour é - crire un mot,

Ma chan - delle est mor - te, je n'ai plus de feu;

Ouv - re - moi ta por - te, pour l'a - mour de Dieu. gent.

1 Au clair de la lune, mon ami Pierrot,
   Prête-moi ta plume, pour écrire un mot,
   Ma chandelle est morte, je n'ai plus de feu;
   Ouvre-moi ta porte, pour l'amour de Dieu.

2 Au clair de la lune Pierrot répondit:
   Je n'ai pas de plume, je suis dans mon lit.
   Va chez la voisine, je crois qu'elle y est,
   Car, dans sa cuisine, on bat le briquet.

3 Au clair de la lune Pierrot se rendort,
   Il rêve à la lune, son coeur bat très fort:
   Car toujours si bonne pour l'enfant tout blanc,
   La lune lui donne son croissant d'argent.

Aiken Drum

Allegro

1. There was a man lived in the moon, lived in the moon, lived

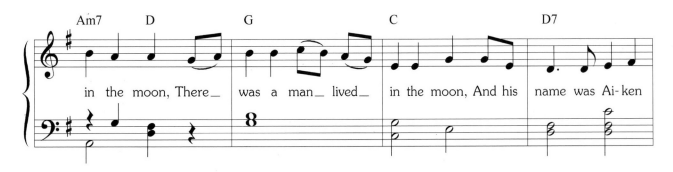

in the moon, There was a man lived in the moon, And his name was Ai-ken

Drum; And he played up-on a la-dle, a la-dle, a

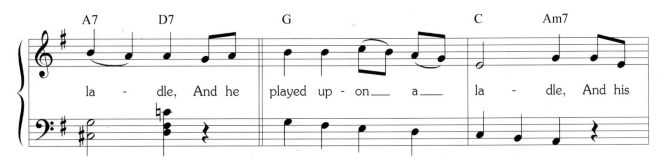

la-dle, And he played up-on a la-dle, And his

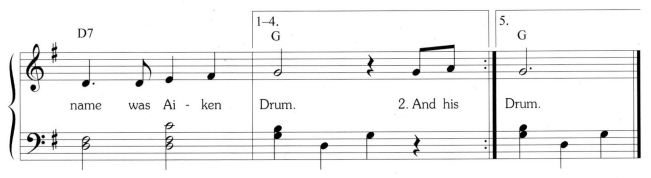

name was Ai-ken Drum. 2. And his Drum.

1 There was a man who lived in the moon,
    lived in the moon, lived in the moon,
There was a man who lived in the moon,
And his name was Aiken Drum;
    And he played upon a ladle, a ladle, a ladle,
    And he played upon a ladle,
    And his name was Aiken Drum.

2 And his hat was made of good cream cheese,
    good cream cheese, good cream cheese,
And his hat was made of good cream cheese,
And his name was Aiken Drum.

    And he played upon a ladle, a ladle, a ladle...

3 And his coat was made of good roast beef,
    good roast beef, good roast beef,
And his coat was made of good roast beef,
And his name was Aiken Drum.

    And he played upon a ladle, a ladle, a ladle...

4 And his buttons were made of penny loaves,
    penny loaves, penny loaves,
And his buttons were made of penny loaves,
And his name was Aiken Drum.

    And he played upon a ladle, a ladle, a ladle...

5 His waistcoat was made of crust of pies,
    crust of pies, crust of pies,
His waistcoat was made of crust of pies,
And his name was Aiken Drum.

    And he played upon a ladle, a ladle, a ladle...

Strawberry Fair

Allegro

As I was go-ing to Straw-ber-ry Fair, Sing-ing, sing-ing,

but-ter-cups and dai-sies, I met a mai-den sel-ling her ware, Fol-de-

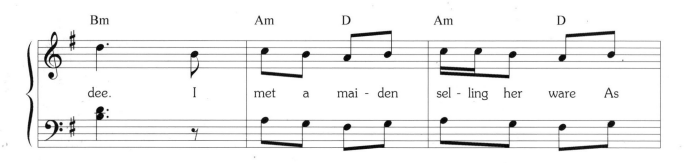

dee. I met a mai-den sel-ling her ware As

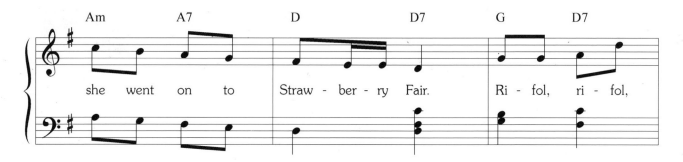

she went on to Straw-ber-ry Fair. Ri-fol, ri-fol,

tol-de-rid-dle-li-do, Ri-fol, ri-fol, tol-de-rid-dle-dee.

50

1 As I was going to Strawberry Fair,
   Singing, singing buttercups and daisies,
   I met a maiden selling her ware,
   Fol-de-dee.
   I met a maiden selling her ware
   As she went on to Strawberry Fair.

        Rifol, rifol, tol-de-riddle-lido,
        Rifol, rifol, tol-de-riddle-dee.

2 As I was going to Strawberry Fair,
   Singing, singing hollyhocks and roses,
   I met a farmer leading his mare,
   Fol-de-dee.
   I met a farmer leading his mare
   As he went down to Strawberry Fair.

        Rifol, rifol, tol-de-riddle-lido,
        Rifol, rifol, tol-de-riddle-dee.

3 As I was going to Strawberry Fair,
   Singing, singing meadowsweet and clover,
   I met a bishop saying a prayer,
   Fol-de-dee.
   I met a bishop saying a prayer
   As she went on to Strawberry Fair.

        Rifol, rifol, tol-de-riddle-lido,
        Rifol, rifol, tol-de-riddle-dee.

Oh, Susanna

Andante

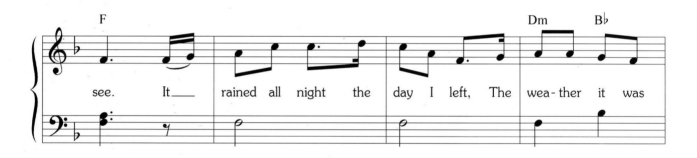

1   I come from Alabama
    With my banjo on my knee;
    I'm going to Louisiana,
    My true love for to see.
    It rained all night the day I left,
    The weather it was dry,
    The sun so hot I froze to death,
    Susanna don't you cry.

Oh, Susanna,
Don't you cry for me.
I've come from Alabama
With my banjo on my knee.

dry, The＿ sun so hot I froze to death, Sus - an - na, don't you

cry. Oh, Sus - an - na, Oh, don't you cry for me. I've＿

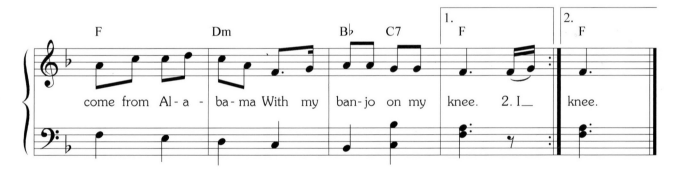

come from Al - a - ba - ma With my ban-jo on my knee. 2. I＿ knee.

2 I had a dream the other night
When everything was still;
I thought I saw Susanna
A-coming down the hill.
The buckwheat cake was in her mouth,
A tear was in her eye;
Says I, "I'm comin' from the South,
Susanna don't you cry."

Oh, Susanna,
Don't you cry for me.
I've come from Alabama
With my banjo on my knee.

Michael, row the boat ashore

Moderato

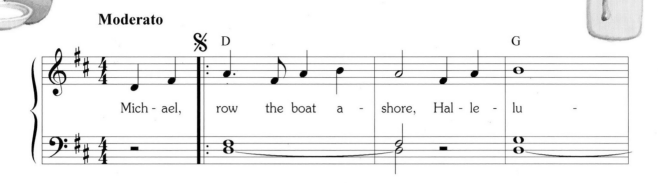

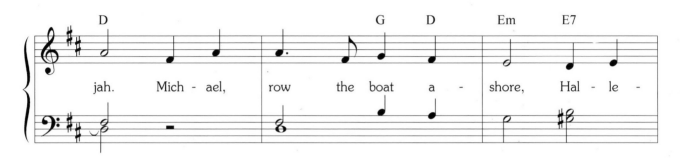

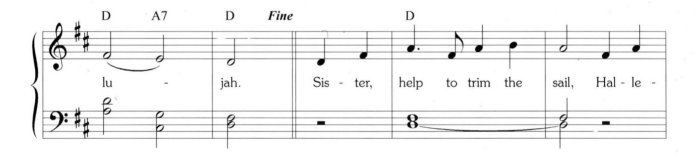

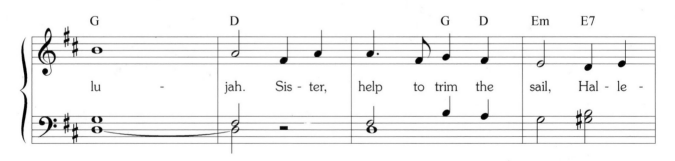

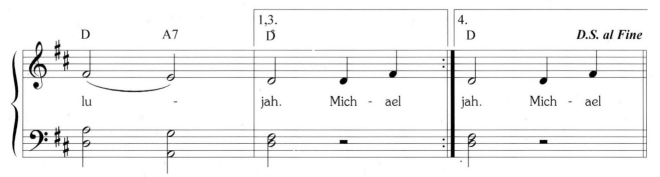

1 Michael, row the boat ashore, hallelujah.
  Michael, row the boat ashore, hallelujah.

2 Sister, help to trim the sail, hallelujah.
  Sister, help to trim the sail, hallelujah.

3 Brother, won't you lend a hand? Hallelujah.
  Steer us to the Promised Land, hallelujah.

4 Children, sing a happy song, hallelujah.
  Help to speed the boat along, hallelujah.

5 River Jordan's deep and wide, hallelujah.
  Milk and honey on the other side, hallelujah.

A froggy went a-courting

Andante

1. A frog-gy went a-court-ing and he did ride, ah - hum, ah -

hum, A frog-gy went a-court-ing and he did ride, ah - hum, ah -

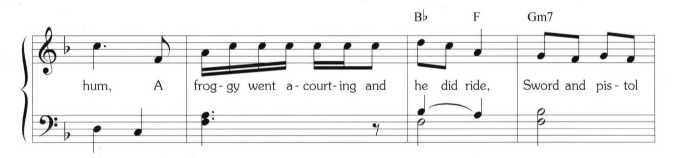

hum, A frog-gy went a-court-ing and he did ride, Sword and pis - tol

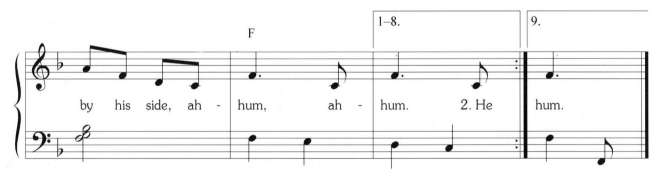

by his side, ah - hum, ah - hum. 2. He | hum.

1 A froggy went a-courting and he did ride, ah-hum, ah-hum,
   A froggy went a-courting and he did ride, ah-hum, ah-hum,
   A froggy went a-courting and he did ride,
   Sword and pistol by his side, ah-hum ah-hum.

2 He rode down to Missy Mouse's door, ah-hum, ah-hum,
   He rode down to Missy Mouse's door, ah-hum, ah-hum,
   He rode down to Missy Mouse's door,
   Where he had been many times before, ah-hum, ah-hum.

3 He took Missy Mouse upon his knee, ah-hum, ah-hum...
   Said, "Miss Mouse, will you marry me?" ah-hum, ah-hum.

4 "Without my Uncle Rat's consent," ah-hum, ah-hum...
   "I wouldn't marry the President," oh-no, oh-no.

5 Uncle Rat laughed and shook his fat sides, ho-ho, ho-ho...
   To think his niece would be a bride, ho-ho, ho-ho.

6 "Where will the wedding breakfast be?" er-hum, er-hum...
   "Way down yonder in the hollow tree," er-hum, er-hum.

7 " What will the wedding breakfast be?" er-hum, er-hum...
   "Fried mosquito and black-eyed pea," yum-yum, yum-yum.

8 They all went sailing across the lake, ah-hum, ah-hum...
   And got swallowed by a big black snake, oh-no, oh-no.

9 There's bread and cheese upon the shelf, er-hum, er-hum...
   If you want any more, you can sing it yourself, er-hum, er-hum.

Home, home on the range

Calmato

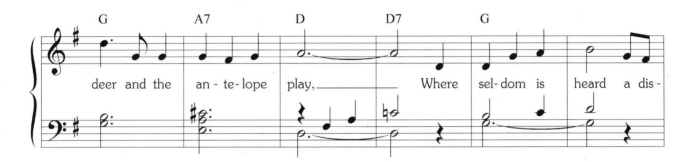

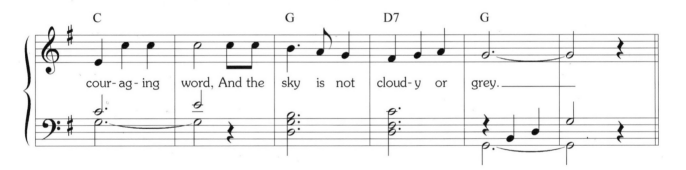

1. Oh, give me a home where the buf-fa-lo roam, Where the deer and the an-te-lope play, Where sel-dom is heard a dis-cour-ag-ing word, And the sky is not cloud-y or grey.

1   Oh, give me a home where the buffalo roam,
Where the deer and the antelope play,
Where seldom is heard a discouraging word,
And the sky is not cloudy or grey.

Home, home on the range.
Where the deer and the antelope play,
Where seldom is heard a discouraging word,
And the sky is not cloudy or grey.

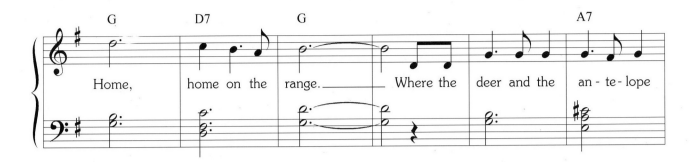

G   D7   G   A7

Home,   home on the   range.   Where the   deer and the   an - te - lope

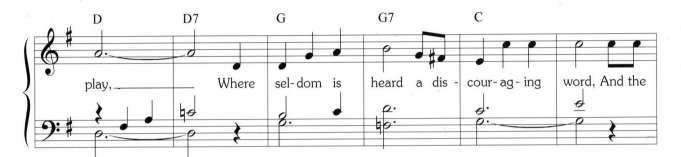

D   D7   G   G7   C

play,   Where   sel - dom is   heard a dis - cour - ag - ing   word, And the

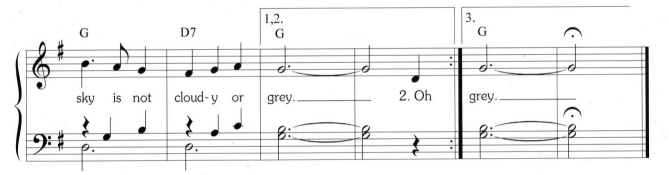

G   D7   1,2. G   3. G

sky   is not   cloud - y or   grey.   2. Oh   grey.

2   Oh, give me a gale in some soft Southern vale,
Where the stream of life joyfully flows,
On the banks of the river, where seldom if ever,
Any poisonous herb-i-age grows.

Home, home on the range...

3   Oh, give me a land where the bright diamond sands
Lie awash in the glittering stream,
Where days glide along in pleasure and song,
And afternoons pass in a dream.

Home, home on the range...

Donkey riding

Allegro

1. Were you ev - er in Que - bec, Stow-ing car - go on the deck?

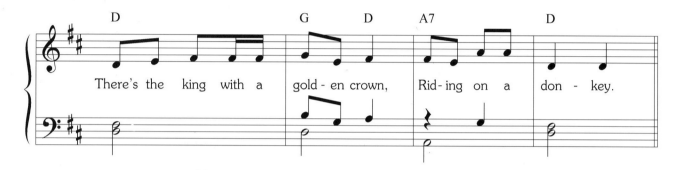

There's the king with a gold - en crown, Rid - ing on a don - key.

Hey, ho, a - way we go, Don - key rid - ing, don - key rid - ing,

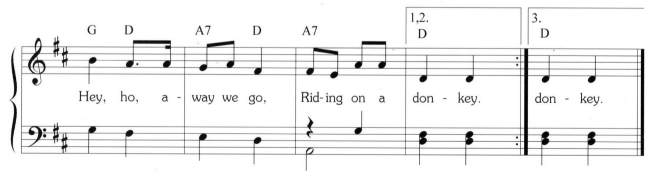

Hey, ho, a - way we go, Rid - ing on a don - key. don - key.

60

1 Were you ever in Quebec,
   Stowing cargo on the deck?
   There's the king with a golden crown,
   Riding on a donkey.

   Hey, ho, away we go,
   Donkey riding, donkey riding,
   Hey, ho, away we go,
   Riding on a donkey.

2 Were you ever in Cape Horn,
   Where it's always fine and warm,
   And seen the lion and the unicorn
   Riding on a donkey?

   Hey, ho, away we go…

3 Were you ever in Cardiff Bay,
   Where the folks all shout, "Hurray!
   Here comes John with his three years' pay
   Riding on a donkey?"

   Hey, ho, away we go…

Lewis Wedding Song

Vivace

Step we gai-ly, on we go, Heel for heel and toe for toe,

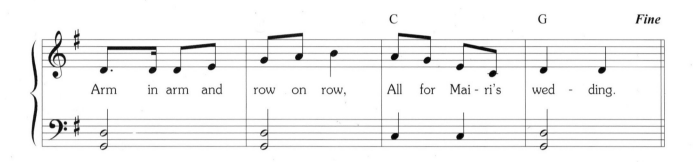

Arm in arm and row on row, All for Mai-ri's wed - ding.

Fine

1. O - ver hill - ways up and down, Myr - tle green and brack - en brown,

Past the shie-lings, through the town; All for sake of Mai - ri.

1,2. G

3. G *D.C. al Fine*

Mai - ri.

Step we gaily, on we go,
Heel for heel and toe for toe,
Arm in arm and row on row,
All for Mairi's wedding.

1   Over hillways up and down,
Myrtle green and bracken brown,
Past the shielings, through the town;
All for sake of Mairi.

Step we gaily, on we go...

2   Red her cheeks as rowans are,
Bright her eye as any star,
Fairest of them all by far,
Is our darling Mairi.

Step we gaily, on we go...

3   Plenty herring, plenty meal,
Plenty peat to fill her creel,
Plenty bonnie bairns as weel;
That's the toast for Mairi.

Step we gaily, on we go...

Shieling is the Scottish word for summer pastures, creel is a basket, and bairns are children.

Guitar chords

The diagrams below show you how to play all the guitar chords used in this book. The vertical lines represent the strings (the lowest on the left) and the horizontal lines are the frets (the top thick line is the nut). The black circles show you where to press the strings, and the numbers beneath tell you which left-hand fingers to use. An o above a string tells you to play it without using any left-hand fingers and an x means you don't play the string at all. A curved line tells you to press a finger across more than one string.

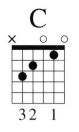
C
x o o
3 2 1

C7
x   x
3 2 4 1

Cm
x x x
3 2 1

D
x x o
1 3 2

D7
x x o
2 1 3

Dm
x x o
2 3 1

Dm7
x x o
2 1 1

D7sus4
x   x
2 3 4 1

Eb
x x x
1 3 2

E7
o o o o
2 1

Em
o   o o o
1 2

Em7
o o o o o
1

F
x x x
2 1 1

F7
1 3 1 2 1 1

G
o o o
2 1   3

G7
o o o
3 2   1

Gm
1 3 4 1 1 1

Gm7
x x
1 1 1 1

A
x o   o
1 2 3

A7
x o o o
1   2

Am
x o   o
2 3 1

Am7
x o o o
2   1

Bb
x x x
3 4 1

Bm
x x x
3 2 1

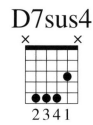
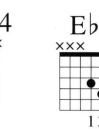
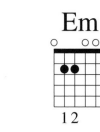
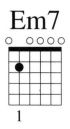
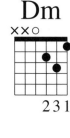
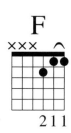

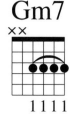
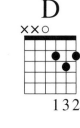

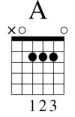
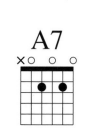
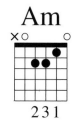
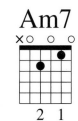
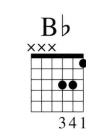
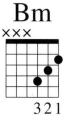